THE SCIENCE BEHIND... BASKETBALL

ALIX WOOD

Enslow PUBLISHING

Published in 2023 by Enslow Publishing, LLC
2544 Clinton Street, Buffalo, NY 14224

Produced for Enslow Publishing by Alix Wood Books
Designed and illustrated by Alix Wood
Edited by Eloise Macgregor

Photo credits: 5, 12, 15, 19, 21, 23, 25, 27, 29 © AdobeStock Images;
11 © Aspenphoto/Dreamstime.com; All illustrations © Alix Wood

Cataloging-in-Publication Data
Names: Wood, Alix.
Title: Basketball / Alix Wood.
Description: New York : Enslow Publishing, 2023. | Series: The science behind... | Includes glossary and index.
Identifiers: ISBN 9781978533035 (pbk.) | ISBN 9781978533059 (library bound) | ISBN 9781978533066 (ebook)
Subjects: LCSH: Basketball--Juvenile literature. | Sports sciences--Juvenile literature.
Classification: LCC GV885.1 W66 2023 | DDC 796.323--dc23

Printed in the United States of America

CPSIA compliance information: Batch #CWENS23: For further information contact Enslow Publishing LLC, at 1-800-398-2504.

Unfortunately, accidents can happen during any sport. Wear suitable clothing and follow all safety advice. Do not try the skills in this book without supervision from a trained adult expert.

Contents

Welcome, Pronk!

Pronk has lots of energy. His friends say he should try for the basketball team. He's very excited. He watches the team warm up.

Pronk is a robot, and robots need clear, scientific instructions. He hopes the team can explain everything in a scientific way, so he understands.

THE SCIENCE

Does science have much to do with basketball? It really does! Science **forces**, such as **gravity**, affect how the ball, and your body, move.

Gravity is the force that pulls everything toward the center of Earth. It's why the ball, and you, come back down to the ground every time.

THE SKILLS

Catching a pass

1. Relax and slightly bend your knees. Hold your hands up, shoulder-width apart. Spread your fingers, palms facing the ball.

2. To catch a high ball, raise your hands with fingers pointing to the ceiling. To catch a low ball, point your fingers to the floor.

3. Step toward the pass. This makes it hard for defenders to steal it. As you catch the ball, move your hands in the direction the ball was traveling.

Learning to Catch

One of the team throws a ball to Pronk. At first, it travels straight and fast. Then it slows and drops a little. Pronk only just manages to catch it!

THE SCIENCE

Scientist Isaac Newton's laws of motion help us understand why moving objects behave like they do. His first law says a still object will stay still, and a moving object will keep moving, unless an **external** force acts on it.

Two forces are acting on the basketball. The force of gravity pulls it down to Earth. Air pushes against the ball, too, causing a force known as **drag**.

His teammate, Harriet, shouts, "Get in a triple-threat!" Pronk has no idea what that is. Harriet shows him how to hold the ball. She says that now, the other team can't guess if he is going to dribble it, shoot it, or pass it!

THE SKILLS

Triple-threat position

1. Place your feet shoulder-width apart, with knees slightly bent, and one foot slightly forward.

2. Hold the ball close to one hip, as though ready to shoot. Keep your elbows out, to defend the ball.

3. Try fooling a defender. Look as if you are going to shoot, then pass the ball instead.

Shooting Some Hoops

The team shouts, "Shoot!" Pronk throws the ball. It goes toward the hoop, but it falls to the ground just too soon. The team tells him he needed to throw it with a little more force.

THE SCIENCE

Basketball players need to use just the right amount of force when they shoot. Too much, or too little, and the ball will not go in the hoop.

Newton's second law says the greater the **mass** (or weight) of an object, the more force you need to move it. A basketball has more mass than a beach ball, so you need to use more force to throw it. Basketball players learn how much force to give the ball through hours of practice.

THE SKILLS

Shoot using B.E.E.F.

1. B is for balance. Stand with your feet shoulder-width apart. Have one foot slightly in front, pointing toward the basket.
2. E is for elbow. Keep your elbow in, directly under the ball. A wobbly elbow can send the ball off-target.
3. The second E is for eyes. Keep your eyes on the target. Aim for the middle of the back of the rim.
4. F is for follow-through. Snap your wrist and push down with your thumb, index, and middle finger. Hold that position until the ball reaches the hoop.

Bouncing a Pass

The team starts passing the ball to each other by bouncing it on the floor. Pronk tries it, too. His ball hardly bounces up at all, so it doesn't reach his teammate. His friends show him he needs to throw the ball down with more force.

THE SCIENCE

Newton, in his third law of motion, says that every action causes an equal and opposite **reaction**.

As the ball pushes down on the ground, the ground pushes back up on the ball with the same force. The harder it hits the floor, the higher the ball will bounce.

There's another reason a basketball bounces. When a basketball hits the floor, the bottom of the ball flattens, so the space inside the ball gets smaller. This causes the air inside to squeeze together. As the air **expands** again, it gives the bounce more energy!

THE SKILLS

The bounce pass

A bounce pass is really useful if a defender's arm or body is blocking a chest pass. Practice the bounce pass with a friend.

1. Hold the ball with both hands, around chest height. Step forward, and reach out with your arms.
2. Snap your wrists to throw the ball forward and down into the floor. Aim the ball so it hits the ground three-quarters of the way between you and your teammate.
3. Keep moving your arms forward after you let go of the ball. Move them to thigh height.

Dribbling

If you want to move around with the ball, you have to bounce it. That's called dribbling. Pronk watches, as his teammates dribble the ball in a zigzag around some cones. They control the ball so well. Pronk wants to learn how to do it!

THE SKILLS

How to dribble the ball

1. Touch the ball with your fingertips, not your palm. Spread your fingers out across the top of the ball.

2. Get low. Place your feet shoulder-width apart. Bend your knees and sit back a little.

3. Bounce the ball firmly and quickly. As the ball comes up, push it back down using your wrist and forearm. Practice dribbling without looking at the ball.

4. Keep the ball low. The shorter the bounce, the harder it is to steal. Keep your body between the defender and the ball.

THE SCIENCE

Why does a ball that has lost some air not bounce well? The more air **molecules** there are inside, the harder that air will push against the sides when the ball squashes. Air molecules slow down when they get cold. That's why a warm basketball will bounce better than a cold one.

A ball's perfect air pressure is between 7.5 and 8.5 **psi**.

Getting a Grip

As the team dribbles the ball around the room, the ball seems to almost stick to their hands. The balls don't feel sticky, though! Pronk looks closely at his basketball. He knows he couldn't hold a bowling ball with his palm like that.

THE SCIENCE

The bumps on a basketball help your hand grip the ball. How? **Friction**. Friction is when one surface or object rubs against another. Bumps cause more friction than a smooth surface.

Try it. Spread the fingers of one hand over the top of a basketball. Can you lift it straight up?

THE SKILLS

Get more friction

Without friction your feet would just keep sliding along the floor. Too much friction and you would stop dead, which can hurt your knees. Basketball shoes are designed to grip, but allow small slips. This gripping and slipping make the grooves on the sole **vibrate**. This vibration is what makes the squeaks you hear on an indoor court!

To get more grip, wipe any dust and dirt from the bottom of your shoes with a damp cloth. Some players use grip spray on their soles or step on sticky pads before a game or during breaks.

The Need for Speed

The team starts to play a practice game. They dart around the court so fast. The really speedy players always beat the others to the hoop. Pronk finds it hard to keep up. He can see he needs to be quick to be good at basketball.

THE SKILLS

Practice speedy getaways

1. Start in a ready position, on the balls of your feet, with your knees bent. You want your shoulders over your knees, and knees over your toes.
2. Jump forward as far and fast as you can off one foot. Land on the other foot, and stay balanced. Get back in the ready position and try using the other foot.

THE SCIENCE

Speed? **Acceleration**? What's the difference? Speed is how fast or slow an object is moving. Acceleration is an increase in speed. In basketball, quick acceleration is useful when you want to beat an opponent.

Changing Direction

When the team stops dribbling, they each seem as if they have one foot is glued to the ground! They can spin around on this foot to make a shot or a pass. But, they can't move the foot until they no longer have the ball. The spin is called a pivot.

THE SKILLS

Pivot

1. Find a place on the court where the lines form a plus sign (+). Place your pivot foot where the lines cross. Get in a triple-threat position with your heels and elbows up.

2. Move your other foot around, onto the line that your pivot foot was pointing to. Keep the ball of your pivot foot still, but allow the rest of your foot to spin around.

3. Pivot back again. Practice pivoting in the other direction, and switching feet, too.

THE SCIENCE

A pivot is a point around which an object can balance or turn. A wrench handle acts like a **lever** to create the force to turn the nut at the pivot point. Your muscles create the force to turn your body around.

Stopping

The sun comes out, so the team heads to the outdoor court. They practice stopping with the ball. Players are not allowed to travel. Traveling is when you take more than two steps without dribbling the ball.

THE SKILLS

Jump stop

1. From a small hop, land softly on both feet, shoulder-width apart.
2. Keep your knees bent and your head up. Balance your weight equally between both feet.
3. Because you land on both feet at once, you can choose to pivot using either foot.

THE SCIENCE

It is sometimes hard to keep your pivot foot still when you land. That is because of **momentum**. Momentum is the force something has when it is moving.

Your body's momentum means it is still traveling forward even though you have planted your feet on the floor! It is why you fall forward if you stop too fast.

THE SKILLS

Stride stop

1. From a small hop, plant one foot on the floor. Then plant your other foot around shoulder-width apart.

2. Keep your knees bent and your head up. Balance your weight evenly on each foot. Whichever foot landed first must be your pivot foot.

3. A stride stop has more momentum than a jump stop. That means you can carry more energy into your shot or pass.

Defending

Harriet gets the ball and looks like she's about to shoot. Pronk decides to make himself as tall as he can, to stop the shot. He gets on his toes and raises his arms. Harriet dodges to one side. Pronk wobbles as he leans to block her. She scores!

THE SCIENCE

The taller you stand, the higher your **center of gravity** will be. Your center of gravity is the point where your mass is the same, left to right, and top to bottom.

Pronk's center of gravity is just above his waist. Gravity pulls on his heavy head and upper body, making him wobble when he leans.

Bend your knees and stay low when defending in basketball.

A low center of gravity makes you more stable. Having bent knees helps you react faster, too.

THE SKILLS

Closing out

1. When your opponent gets the ball, move quickly toward them. You want to be around an arm's length away.

2. Keep on your toes, with your feet shoulder-width apart and your knees slightly bent.

3. Move your arms around and try to steal the ball, knock away their shot, or block their view.

Angles and Gravity

Pronk watches the team practice shooting baskets. They seem to throw the ball too high. Then, gravity pulls the ball back down. A lot of shots bounce off the rim of the basket.

THE SCIENCE

Objects travel through the air in an **arc**. A ball is more likely to pass through a basketball hoop if the arc is steep. Why? Because the hoop is a large circle shape from above. From a low angle, the hoop becomes smaller and oval-shaped. Because of this, a low ball is more likely to hit the rim.

THE SKILLS

Getting a good angle

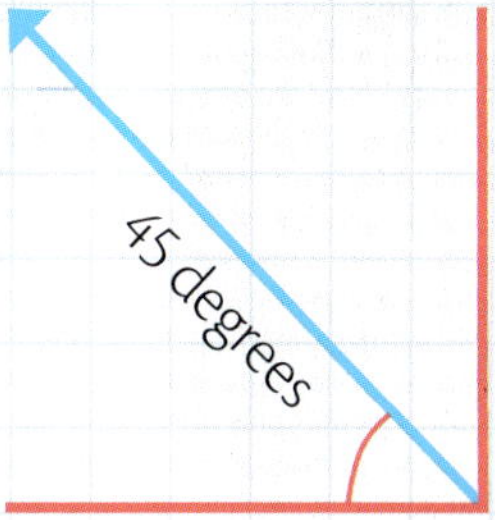

1. Aim to throw the ball at around a 45 degree angle.

2. Try to get the ball so it reaches around 3-4 feet (90-120 cm) above the rim.

3. To get the height, get your elbow above your eyes when you release the ball.

4. Add power to your throw by pushing off the floor with your legs.

Add Some Spin

Some of the shots hit the backboard, and then spin down into the net. It is almost like the net sucks them in as they bounce away from the board!

Pronk thinks that looks cool. He wants to learn to spin the ball next.

THE SKILLS

Creating backspin

Backspin makes the ball spin in an upward direction. When it hits the board, it bounces off in the opposite direction. Try it.

1. Hold the ball with spread fingertips. Position your middle finger in the middle of the ball.
2. With your elbow under the ball, raise your arm and flick your wrist forward. This causes the ball to spin toward you.

THE SCIENCE

It's not just the force of a ball's bounce that produces an equal and opposite reaction. The angle of a bounce does, too. With no spin, a ball will bounce away at the exact opposite angle that it hits an object at.

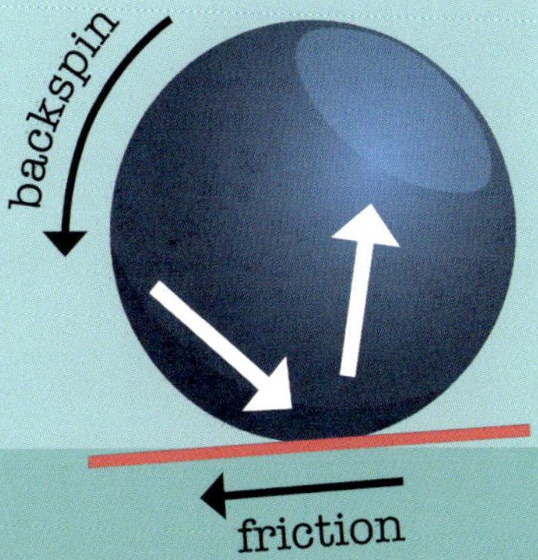

A ball with backspin may bounce at a steeper angle. Friction slows the ball. The spin can make the ball bounce slightly backward. The ball can even change the direction that it spins as it bounces!

Hang Time

Some of the players practice jumping as they shoot a basket. They seem to hang in midair for ages! Then, they slam dunk the ball through the top of the hoop. The jump certainly gets them a perfect angle.

THE SCIENCE

Can you really hang in midair? No, you just seem to. You move fastest at the beginning and end of a jump. In the middle of a jump the pull of gravity slows you, until eventually you stop going up. You pick up speed as you come down again. So, most of your jump time is spent hanging in the top third of the jump!

THE SKILLS

High jump

Before you can learn to slam dunk, you need to be able to jump high.

1. Stand with your feet facing forward, under your hips. Press your knees slightly outward.

2. Squat by bending at your hips and knees. Hold the ball close to your body. It is a good idea to practice with a small ball, such as a tennis ball.

3. Jump up by pushing your feet hard into the floor. At the same time, throw your arms forward and overhead. Reaching up with just one hand usually gets the ball higher than with both hands. Land softly, bending your knees as you land.

Basketball Science Quiz

Do you have basketball science know-how? See if you can answer these questions. The answers are on page 32.

1. What force pulls us toward the ground?
   a) drag b) gravity c) friction

2. When a ball hits the ground, the ground pushes back up on the ball with the same force.
   a) true
   b) false

3. Why do the bumps on a basketball help you grip it?
   a) bumps cause more friction than a smooth surface
   b) the bumps are sticky
   c) bumps cause less friction than a smooth surface

4. If you bounce pass forward with no backspin, what will the ball do?
   a) it will bounce back at you at the same angle
   b) it will bounce away from you at the same angle
   c) it will bounce straight up in the air

Science Words

acceleration an increase in speed.

arc a curved path.

center of gravity the point in an object or person where their weight is balanced.

drag a force which tends to slow the movement of an object through liquid or gas.

expand to grow or increase in size.

external occurring outside.

force the push or pull on something.

friction a force that restricts the movement of two objects sliding along each other.

gravity the force that pulls things toward the center of Earth.

lever a simple machine that uses an effort and a pivot to lift or move objects.

mass how much matter is in an object.

molecules the smallest particles of a substance.

momentum the strength of a moving object.

psi a measurement of pressure, in pounds per square inch.

reaction a response to something that has happened or has been done.

vibrate to move back and forth or from side to side very quickly.

Index

Quiz answers: 1. b) gravity; 2. a) true; 3. a) bumps cause more friction than a smooth surface; 4. b) it will bounce away from you at the same angle